LIVE FROM THE MOOD BOARD

LIVE FROM THE MOOD BOARD

——————————

CANDICE REFFE

ELIXIR PRESS
DENVER, COLORADO

Book design by Steven Seighman
Cover design by Michaela Sullivan

Library of Congress Cataloging-in-Publication Data

Names: Reffe, Candice, author.
Title: Live from the mood board / Candice Reffe.
Description: Denver, Colorado : Elixir Press, [2019] | Winner of the Exilir
Press Annual Poetry Award.
Identifiers: LCCN 2018042546 | ISBN 9781932418705 (alk. paper)
Classification: LCC PS3618.E44594 A6 2019 | DDC 811/.6--dc23 LC record
available at https://lccn.loc.gov/2018042546

First edition: February 2019

10 9 8 7 6 5 4 3 2 1

for Ed & Zeke

for my parents, Herman & Lucille

CONTENTS

THE DROP RACK

THE SAME HARMONIC

Life is the only way to
get covered in leaves

—WISŁAWA SZYMBORSKA
(Translated by Stanisław Barańczak and Claire Cavanagh)

He stood transfigured before himself.
How he played it out, ah, played! rainbowed! greened!

—GOTTFRIED BENN
(Translated by David Paisley)

Introduction

Most first books of poetry are autobiographical, for obvious reasons. In particular, lyric poems enfold autobiography at their cores, minute autobiographies of consciousness. Any dedicated museum goer has encountered self-portraits by Dürer, Van Gogh, Cindy Sherman, Robert Mapplethorpe and countless others, whether realized in graphite, paint or pixels. Auteurs as varied as François Truffaut, Agnès Varda and Andrei Tarkovsky included autobiography as an element in their oeuvres. Artists are their own most irresistible, convenient and omnipresent subject matter, yet poets of insight and sensitivity discover continuities ensuring that readers are able to connect with, be moved by, their perceptions and time-stamped experiences.

The title of Candice Reffe's collection *Live from the Mood Board* suggests not only the vivacity and changeable emotions of her poems, but gets directly at an element that makes this rather autobiographical first book quite unique. Instead of focusing on an event of personal crisis, or the illness or death of a loved one, or the poet's experiences with her first family (as do so many debut collections), Reffe's book reflects on the life of a professional working in fashion design and merchandising—domain of the mood board, the sales cycle, the runway, the conference room. At the same time, the collection charts the yearning and frustrations of a woman whose drive to channel her energies toward making art is stymied by quotidian demands of making a living. Reffe's images and metaphors depict an insider's view of the fashion world, no doubt foreign to most poets and poetry-readers, with originality and perceptive depth. Employees returning from a winter holiday register "freedom as a luxury we're about to pay tax on. Each / of us entered into a cell on a spreadsheet, / confined by its border at desks or meetings." Charged with writing encouraging jargon to spur on her colleagues, one executive grieves the inaccessibility of her own creative logos, her restriction in the corporate "pen": "I flit my dream's hallways & elevators in stockings & suit."

A tidy band of exceptions proves the rule that published poets in the contemporary United States work in the academy, publishing industry, or arts-oriented non-profits. The stray pediatricians, advertising execs and standup comedians who also write poetry collections jump quickly to mind by force of the charm of their rarity. Reffe's poems likewise exude a freshness and pleasing oddity partially due to her ability to identify and develop aspects of humanity and humor in what some outsiders might assume is an antiseptic corporate vacuum. Reffe gives readers a curious, engrossing perspective on this distinctive pocket of the New York City business world and its corollary components, including the commute, the business trip, the weekend detox after a month of frantic crunch-time days.

Taking us "where I sink / a needle into another day's groove, to the record turning," Reffe weaves images and metaphors involved with design and clothes-making into many of her free verse poems. She compares a traffic cop to a yellow jacket in an extended metaphor that spotlights the woman's narrow waist, her chartreuse and black uniform. In an airport vignette, Sarah Jessica Parker's twins are revealed to be "bespoke, bestowed" as the amusingly envious speaker's sighting of this most fashionable traveler gives rise to "gauzy wishes, cloud-colored florets / blown back into a backyard dandelion." Elsewhere, the speaker presents her "larcenous sorrow zipped in a wet suit." Another vivid fashion-infused image is her "K-Mart mother / in a seal coat that shifts from dark to light & back again / with a child's pawed stroking." The section-length poem "The Drop Rack" explicitly contends with synchronicities between the mindset and activities of a fashion professional and those of an artist. Consciousness is prized, recognized as "hand-knit minutes."

Despite the professional nexus evident also in section titles such as "Earthling in Transit" and "Human Resources," this book is far from being a narrative-heavy, matter-of-fact account of events in a businesswoman's nonstop work life. Many of Reffe's poems make forays into the intricacies of consciousness as a woman explores contingent versions of self, some disturbing—a dog/woman futilely sniffing a mother's bones, a penis-biting snake—others delightful in their singularity: "I wouldn't mind being trees walking" and "I'd rather be the view of town from shore seen / from a dad's shoulders." Often, this speaker who wants "to un-become" herself tries out flight in the guise of a bird. Avian references abound throughout, one of several image sequences the poet deploys with artful, judicious poise. Rather than tiring of birds, readers are likely to appreciate the myriad ways they inhabit poems such as "Kink in the Polar Vortex: Letter to my Husband," in which both spouses morph into lousy pigeons, "shingled wing to wing on the lee / ridge."

Perhaps loneliness drives the speaker's impulse toward zoanthropy, another persistent trope, for this emotion shades the mood of several of the poems, from the child playing by herself in "Self Portrait in a Rental Kitchen" to the poignant portrait of a wife experiencing psychological alienation despite the presence of her husband in the same room, quarantined by his ear buds. Some of Reffe's most empathetic and passionate lyrics consider the fates of lab animals and victims of industrial farming.

The pleasure of this collection accrues in Reffe's deft, unique images but also in her harmonic and effective work with sound, amplifying the image with repetition, slant rhyme and assonance. Take for example: ". . . she'll become a rack of bones, bone / in my mouth, my mouth / a ship's bow water-trilled, a black- / lipped dog-mouth, foaming." Conceiving one office scene as a metaphoric soundstage, Reffe plays up the point with alliteration: "Each voice a string plucked, a lack amplified / from childhood. The past polyphonic / in the present: someone's operatic / mother, TV-remote father. Contrapuntal / in conference rooms, copy / rooms, corridors, layered into every office / encounter, counteracting the main melody, the actual / work day." This passage also demonstrates the poet's skillful, multivalent line breaks.

Reffe sustains the velocity of the book with her sophisticated soundscapes and surprising metaphors, highlighting conjunctions of the clothing trade and aesthetics in the mind of a woman immersed both in fashion's color scales and the poet's practice of observing natural and built worlds. She notes "the chromatic / collision of beauty and violence" in the smashed body of a squirrel before riffing on the history of red dye, its covert ingredients of arsenic and the cochineal of crushed insects. Supple syntax and subtle variations in poetic form also add to this debut collection's complexity and polish. Readers across age ranges and geographical and economic situations are likely to resonate with the struggle toward psychic and professional liberation that builds momentum throughout this book—the sense of consciousness taking wing to escape the mundane, as the conflicted self "becomes a hallelujah."

—*Kathleen Winter, contest judge*

EARTHLING IN TRANSIT

The Cop's a Winged Insect

                              Debating
whether to sting? Disaffected jaywalkers—
                              our human confusion

        sugaring our speed down the street—don't we
need to be stopped, to be stung
                              into feeling?

        Or be supped on, the brew that is us
liquefied like a grub or a fly and fed
                              back to us, so we

        taste what we're made from? Waist narrow
as a yellow jacket's, the cop's a queen aglow

        in her chartreuse TRAFFIC t-shirt tucked into
regulation black pants. Her blonde bangs

                translucent as wings signal us—and it's then,
        as I cross, I see
not insects, but birds about to fly
                              from her tattooed wrists

        into clouds dazzling as milk teeth.

The Zoanthropist

I'm just another carnivore with good cleavage.

My indentured eyelashes, under halogen lights, to & fro the 9 to 5 catwalk.

I eat applause like red meat. I like it blue & bloody.

When no one claps, I preen myself with my beak.

Each morning, I dip my fingertips into an unwashed orifice & sniff.

In my salty scent the universe effloresces.

I'm a disco ball dizzy with facets.

The tornado inside the turquoise beach dress: blue mummy in the sun.

I'm the sun pucked through a cloud's mouth.

I'm the snake who bit Kwabena Nkrumah's penis in a public toilet.

I'm Mohammed Salmodin's teeth who bit the snake back.

I'm the god of small favors. Regurgitated, the lost laundry sock.

I'm a princeling on the nightshift, stock boy, eager mall greeter *hello, hello, ma'am.*

I'm the shopper shaking the subverted spokes of her mutinous umbrella.

I'm her black & blue pinky, snapped at the airport hotel for cancelled flights.

I'm Jesus is Lord signed in steam across a mirror in an Embassy Suite.

I'm my own erstwhile emptiness, hell-bent on returning.

The promiscuous memory of a minor divinity. Forgotten four digits of a
     social security.

When I'm ready, I'll become a pigeon & retire to the sea's delectable landfill.

Then a butterfly, so I can taste with my feet.

Then a pig whose orgasm lasts 30 minutes.

Then a bull frog. So I can sing without sleep.

Self Portrait in a Rental Kitchen

1.

Rowed through five days of rain, my mind a spin-dial
ratcheted click by click shut.
                                        The boats in my mind
clocking east, a muckle of black-backed gulls

electrolytically lit, bunting the wind, an iridescence
that suggests it might be
                                        possible to climb my skull's seaside
cliff on cramponed feet into these hand-knit minutes.

2.

But time shape-shifts like a dune & what is buried
resurfaces: eavesdropped
                           notes of two-fingered
chopsticks on a toy piano, metal jacks flung

like sleep-away-camp stars, a white furred
terrier stuffed with an
                           approachable happiness,
hauled everywhere by a child who always & almost

only played by herself—misfit,
even after I fit in, after
                           transmigrating to California
at thirteen, a freed pilgrim. Even after crossing

the equator & crossing back, my fixed abode an
isolation tank, a basement
                           drenched with a mother's
tears, her hand-knit suffering calling.

3.

Even now, long after her passing, an alarm's fluorescent
beep jacks off—erratic—staccato—incessant—insistent,
                                                    I'm still
wired-in, the present moment short-
                            circuiting, corkscrewing

like the pitch pine out here, each of the cone's scales
with its barb curved inward as
                            a toe nail, habitual
as loneliness.

One of the Regulars

What more can I ask than to be known by the barista
        at Prêt a Manger, Vanessa, who rings my order

before my unoiled lips open. Her optimistic pigtail tick-tocks
        from her maroon baseball cap, white star stamped

above its lid stamping her Caffeinator of the Universe.
        What more than to be known by the goateed ticket

taker at Amtrak's New Haven station, his crossword smile,
        the Bodhisattva who punches my name as I glide

to his window—no reservation number, no I.D needed.
        Known also by the security guard who holds

open the door signed Do Not Open, as I wheel
        my suitcase through. Who I know as Steve of

the brass-buttoned navy-jacket, gum-chewed *Good Morning*,
        Oz of stuck-elevators, red-button emergencies.

Who knows if his misplaced dreams too pressed
        Pause, the way the wind's winged maple seeds

pause just before guttering. Mine spun up by the bell boy's
        Hello Beautiful: I'm one of his regulars.

The rain too praises my uncharacteristic cheer in the form
        of an orange umbrella, the tarred heavens breaking

open to greet all earthlings in transit this morning,
           including me, because in between Here & There

isn't Nowhere. It's where I sink
           a needle into another day's groove, the record turning.

High Wattage

Why not bathe in the atmospheric glow of Sarah Jessica Parker
        the day after I spot her & the day after that
                one of the phytoplankton blooming in her wake

as she chased her toddlers, toddler one
        & toddler two down the airplane aisle, her light bulb
                smile switched on at no one particular, pursued

by powdery whispers: moths fidgeting from every mouth,
        it's Sarah Jessica… If it weren't for our
                seat belts, we'd prostrate ourselves before her,

crossing fingers fame was contagious, or at least adhesive
        & would redefine us the way pine pollen's
                yellow fluorescence highlights the convex hood

of every car in spring, *vroom, vroom.* Why not google Sarah J
        (& her menschy husband Matthew Broderick) the following
                jet-lagged morning. Divulged: the toddlers

bespoke, bestowed: even the famous require a surrogate
        to reboot their family. After all it's not
                their fault they're famous, is it? So by extension, not

my fault I'm not, or that the tiny breeze that trails Ms. Parker,
        carries with it my gauzy wishes, cloud-colored florets
                blown back into a backyard dandelion. Why not

let her fame become mine, heretofore unrealized,
        though I am a famous mother to my son, a famous shopper
                at Cathy Cross where I spend my bundle.

Cathy's not famous either, or famous only in our little town
　　　　for silken blazers, spaghetti strap summer dresses &
　　　　　　　　cropped linen box-tops, like the one Ms. Parker breast-

strokes into when she de-planes. At baggage claim, chance
　　　　places her beside me: our belongings, equal,
　　　　　　　　slalom the silver chute, spin clockwise, while an older

woman (grandmother? fake or real?) asks "How did
　　　　the kids do?" And Sarah J reports—*nota bene*:
　　　　　　　　even famous offspring barf on airplanes.

What a bummer, I want to say sloughing off my shyness,
　　　　where did you buy your sweater—in this
　　　　　　　　instance of chance, instant best friends.

But I don't.
　　　　I don't even look at her,
　　　　　　　less than
　　　　　　　　　　two feet between her life & mine.

I Become the West Coast

When the blood divided my father's heart,
       I too parted, like the Red Sea for my sister's tears,

my brother's. My own, bubble-wrapped by a mother
       (dead too) whose tears were her instrument—

the reedy music that drew me down
       down to the briny basement, where she sang

the drowned notes of *Only the Lonely.* Her arced
       shoulders, her unrequited hair carved

like a figurehead's on a prow. I was her bitt,
       her bowline, her fore & aft mooring. Decades

poured past us. By the time I left I'd become
       like the West Coast, an unprecedented drought.

My larcenous sorrow zipped in a wet suit. No matter
       the tremor, in my California, no quake.

Or Teddy Roosevelt's Hand On the Pilgrim Monument

I'd rather be the view of town from shore seen
from a dad's shoulders than
                              the view seen by a strand
of eel grass, caught on a flip flop the horizon

slides toward me. Greedy for warmth,
arms soldered to thighs to deck,
                              I shanghai the last scrap
of sunlight a gull parts from clouds. I wouldn't mind

being the gull's stuttered belly
instead of grooved
                    waves engraved
on the sea bed, their glossy redundancy.

I wouldn't want to be that sign sunk in sand,
a semaphorist warning all swimmers,
                                    but the swimmer who
to hell with it dove in, the pleasured pull of arm

over arm, of going somewhere
in water. Or going nowhere,
                            naffing about on a yellow raft.
I wouldn't want to be that beach chair expelled

from sunlight, folded in on itself.
I already know the taste
                         of salt-crumbed rust.
I'd rather not forget the view from the 116th

step of the Pilgrim Monument, shore bowing
to town, taste of the New World.
                                 If I had to choose
right now, I'd be one of the two trees hoisted shoulder-height

by a woman seen from the yard side of a privet hedge,
not the woman, but the moving
                               tops of trees all that's visible—
I wouldn't mind being trees walking.

Pilgrimage

For a Spiritus pizza slice, pass by Don
who is Dolly, in her flawless brunette flip,
fuchsia sheath. Pasted to her lipsticked

lower lip, a cigarette smokes itself. Despite
the day's gender dialect, she calls
herself a TV. Switched on, her pelvis

transmits the beat carried on currents from
the A-House to Commercial Street.
Hi honey, hi baby, echoes west to east.

Two boys in tight, black & white striped
briefs circle their hips like hula-hoopers,
the fifties girl my hips tried to be.

Everyone comes to the sea. Here
we're equal. The straight, overweight
inlanders, the skinny ones like me.

Here for the taffy, here to gawk, here
to seek. Even the town's cock-jockey
Republicans in their oversized houses

overlooking the beach. The caricaturist
captures us all who overtake the street.
Not a car can get down it.

P-town's our mecca. Our holiness
is precarious. Shoulder to shoulder,
we could become a stampede.

Keyed Up

The sky's empty as a waiting room this morning:
antiseptic & fluorescent.
                    Behind its passive haze, it seethes.
            It wants to snow. I want it to.
    Want snow to disappear
the scorched December lawns strict straw-colored
            grass uptight as military hair
            just cut at starched attention.

    Disappear the flowerbed's slashed mouth
            dark as discarded coffee grinds
                    narrow as a neighbor's coffin.
                    Want it to blizzard, to blaze, to blot, to blare
            telephone wires lassoed, houses &
    cars concussed, each tree's bare limbs
    spelled out & memorized.
                            I want to be memorized.

    Instead I'm a vagrant in my own house, parked
under an absent-minded pile of pilly blankets in a vestibule.

                    I want the snow to snow inside,
                                            obliterate
            my unpaid bills unread magazines undone
        to-do list un-churned laundry, my funk
    sticky as the sleeve of oil adorning
last night's dirty dishes.
    I want the snow to make my
            tea-stained teeth bright again
                    my funk shook off like icy driblets by a dog who's
                    rolled in just-snowed snow.
                                    I want

to un-become myself, become
the snow instead: Poured interruption,
my self played like
a scale by snow, my ivories, ebony sharps
& flats fingered, my life
my dazzling emptiness,
improvised.

You Again.

After thirty years. What are you doing here?
        You overflowing, overflown like the tub water's seep
                through sheet rock. Its echoed stain

weeps the letters of your last name—mine too—
        blocky capitals magic-markered across your right calf: REFFE.
           Wired to your right toe, your nametag.

Thirty years ago I looked down on the hull of you, the not
        you of you, you hawsered
               to a stainless steel table, barnacled, impatient

to be oars-in scudding to the afterlife. When you surface again,
        you're refashioned whole, lopped breasts sutured
              back to your body. Again the K-Mart mother

in a seal coat that shifts dark to light & back again
        with a child's pawed stroking. Pink satin dress
            tied with a bow, pink satin heels, pink smudge

of your lips staining my cheek, a ghost passing.
        You might as well be fog burning through the fringed
            blades of a palm tree, or one of your

precious oranges enthralled with its own reflection
        in the burred grass, the burning sun of a negligible planet.
           When you resurface, you surface at my age, so

I look you in the eye—now I'm a mother too, I know
        what you know. What do you
           think of that, ghost?

Kink in the Polar Vortex: Letter to My Husband

If we were beaked creatures—lousey pigeons, perhaps
      feathers swelling with air, inflating

with our fellow pigeons, shingled wing to wing on the lee
      ridge of a beach-house roof, New Year's Day snowstorm—

or buffleheads, burrowed, oily feathers
      converged with the pack, local black-backs driven
            by freak cold into one viscous blot on the bay.

If we were beaked creatures we'd recognize
      when the atmosphere's unstable. We'd have
         known it was coming, as they did.

Yesterday, the bay emptied of birds.
      Ducks peeled from water to shore, assembled
         by stairs you & I use
            to walk into the sea in summer.

Now, on the windward side of the New Year,
      in the frigid, elliptical flow, the temperature rising

then dropping, you & I drop
      into our own metabolic torpor.
        We ride it out solo:

A woman looks up from her book, pulled
      by the snow's diagonal spill across water.

That's loneliness, she thinks: A life
        lived as a view observed out a window
            or turning it over she considers
               as the viewer.

Back turned, a man brews coffee, singly tuned
        to what's falling through ear buds the color of snow,

inside the precision of beans, grind, roiling water.
        The darkness extracted
            congruent with his.

Like this, the afternoon passes.
        The birds persist in their feathered intersection.

        Husband, it's cold in here.

Her Bones Are So Fine Even the Bed Can Break Them

1.

We don't need an osteomancer to mark & toss them like dice,
      to divine she'll become a rack of bones, bone
          in my mouth, my mouth
               a ship's bow water-trilled, a black-

lipped dog mouth, foaming.
          Boneheaded death: with little meat between,
     my mother's bones
        click-clack
          their castanets

        till she's a rack of nothingness, unsniffable
          by my 220 million dog smell cells.

2.

Mother, I've come for my last kiss, but you are not here.

Who is this you-not-you, still life in the Slumber Room, last-
        goodbye room, so long, farewell, *auf wiedersehen…*
                                        Why not
                break into song? You loved a good show tune.

Why not croon you back
        into this arctic auditorium?
                                A low-watt moon rises
                        over your hair—over the top
                sheet I draw off you.

I trace the scar where your
        nipple once erupted like checkerberry through snow crust.
                I scratch & sniff, but your scent

refuses release. Eau de Lucille,
        Eau de Ma Mère: Evaporated.
                                I'm a stray, dead-set to excavate

the nut of you. Tiny kisses, furious kisses:
                                nostrils, eyelids,
                abridged lips. I trace your
                        ear whorls with my sandpaper tongue. *Mama.*

                                But you've hightailed it.
        You've left your body for good, Mother:
                What good is it to me?

Between index & thumbnail I tweeze
                        a white hair from your pillow, shove

it in my pocket. Goodbye
                to your big toe with its toe-tag.
                                        Goodbye to your calf magic-
markered with our last name. Goodbye to your
flesh slab splayed like a plucked
                        chicken gliding on steel wheels to the roaster.

3.

If I were a modern Hindu, I'd punch Go & watch through glass
  jet flame consume your torso,
       your seas evaporate, tissues tighten, vaporize
        skin wax, discolor, blister, split.

Charred muscles flex & limbs extend:
      Are you coming back to life, my Frankencille?

  Your bones, your lovely, spongy bones, the last to go.
    They calcify & flake.
      Two or three hours at most till you roll out

the other side. Your sum total?
      Approximately seven pounds of ash—

gray gravel coarse as the winding ridge deposited by
  meltwater under a glacier: You've become
       an esker in a copper box.

4.

We're down to the nitty-gritty at the boneyard.

Down to us kids settling accounts with twin copper boxes:
one for the columbarium, one for us.

Down to the mortuary director's nails buffed
as the ivory brocade hush, when he confers
like a diploma
box number two into my sister's hands.

She shakes the box like a maraca:
"This is it?"

5.

If I were Yanomani I'd pulverize your bones & teeth inside a log:
      Remove remains. Rinse log with plantain soup. Drink.

      I'd be your twenty-something endocannibalist.

6.

Thirty years past, I'm still grubbing for your gone bone, bent
by brightness this wintery morning.

                                    Sequential time bent too: Returned

from death's encore at Goodwill
your flowered apron

                        again tied round your waist—perhaps
still tied round someone's waist, if not

                                  disintegrating as waste in landfill.

7.

"Do you believe the dead & living speak?"

We're in our bodies, spooning on your sick bed.
Death is spooning with us.

Death has no eardrum, but like the lizard, detects
our hum through its jawless jawbone.

You touch your faceted ear tips, your K-Mart diamonds:
"These will be our radio transmitters."

The day you leave your body, I screw the earrings in.
Come in, come in. Over.

Nothing.

Is it the discount diamond?
Or in death are you restricted to higher

frequencies than human ears can hear?
Arf. Arf.

Below Freezing, Yet

A black ant draws a dotted line across
a stainless steel counter,
                    dividing winter from spring.
By June, an ant campaign will seethe in the kitchen

& I'll concoct a fatal perfume from honey & borax,
but now, right now, this ant
                    first of the season, thaws
my frostbit funk & resuscitates my attention—

for a nanosecond I become a hallelujah.
Another winter poured
                    off like whistling water,
the tea leaves mum. A coatless

fortune teller reclines under a budding quince
in the grass sheen, imitating
                    a cloud. Easy
to exclaim over

the hyacinth's blades banging like a lung inside
the earth's rib cage,
                    improvising a sleeveless future.
But that's the sound of

time going by—whiff of the past on
113th Street an electric
                    current passing through my
present body, decades collapsing like a one-row

squeezebox, an operatic rendition of my life
by accordion, one choice
                     ricocheting off another choice, one
kiss off another kiss, California sky coinciding, colliding with

New York sky, all the I's I've ever been an echo of an
echo of an echo, become
                     the originating note again—
the song inside the bird, the bird inside the song.

HUMAN RESOURCES

The Executive Assistant's Astral Existence

"I'm a bit perplexed by all the attention paid to me,
when it is the comet that deserves the credit,"
　　　　—Yuji Hyakutake

I look down from the astral plane with a bigger-
　　　　than-boss-size view of the office, each cubby &
　　　　　　　　copier, every working soul's contacts & calendar.

That's why I took this job:
　　　　An Exec Assistant, I can glide anywhere—I'm
　　　　　　　　supposed to be invisible. Because virtuous,

cheerful, efficient, easy to slide from the surface
　　　　and watch the spheres turn in this
　　　　　　　　human world made of Chap-stick,

breath mints, spare pair of glasses
　　　　so sight is never misplaced.
　　　　　　　　Pills white as snow, potent enough

to parry an avalanche of panic. My boss
　　　　stashes a mirror that magnifies & red lipstick
　　　　　　　　so her nine-to-five mouth speaks the same

dialect as the other mouths. Up here in the ether, no
　　　　one is speaking; I can hear everything. Some
　　　　　　　　are logomaniacs, some can't get a word in.

Each voice a string plucked, a lack amplified
　　　　from childhood. The past polyphonic
　　　　　　　　in the present: someone's operatic

mother, TV-remote father. Contrapuntal
in conference rooms, copy
rooms, corridors, layered into every office

encounter, counteracting the main melody, the actual
work day. No one's exempt, no matter how
lofty their title. I grab my boss coffee,

no sugar, board my astral vehicle every morning,
enter my winged coordinates
in my eternal reminders. From up here,

I hear the hurt ticking in every heart hired.
How can I remind them we're
also composed of the stars, the fifth element,

an inaudible harmony. Some of them never
bother to greet me, never call me by name:
Fortunia Antares Hyakutake.

Not a Mouth Wants to Open

after the Christmas closing through New Year's.

In the city, even the snow's supervised: heavy
        machinery flows, every avenue's calculated: *Salt*

is King! the mayor declares. At One
        Union Square the clock spins militarily

to the second, out fifteen digits, a slots
        the city keeps feeding. Steam

exhales through a grate—a god-
        size breath I walk willingly into before

my heavy head nods on its stalk
        at the office. Even the dedicated don't want

to be here after two weeks duty-free. Freedom
        a luxury we're about to pay tax on. Each

of us entered into a cell on a spreadsheet,
        confined by its border at desks or meetings.

Together we make a beautiful formula.
        Logarithmic, the sum of us exponential

        as leaves flown back into trees.

A Fifth Century Chicken Returns to Address Her Descendants

Yes I'm talking to you, at Ash-O-Ley Acres,
flock "with the sunlight." Your farmer

insists you flap your wings "happily."
Tell me, hens, are you happy?

As compared to you, static in the back,
in the barn's dark—weighed down

by your breasts, your legs continuing to
snap? (Jim Perdue says he'll tinker

with that.) And you, in Jersey, Florida,
featherless from endlessly resting on

your ammonia-soaked shit, I come

from the graveyard to call you
from your pens, your aviaries. In my century

we're not even yellow. Eggs? Laid only
occasionally. I ate what my lord ate,

bless the castle, bless him. When his time came,
worthy as a ruby, I opened

my throat. As in life, to lie
beside him. Among humans,

I was free: they did not
would not
eat me.

My Life Shrinks to the Size of a Midge

The one that flew into my mouth, its wet wings banging
my throat cage, the bloated scent of sea, low decibel
feeling something's coming inexorable as a red
dress, ruched storm cloud contracting as my
face contracts my face a motor boat idling
at high tide, cocktail hour collecting a swarm
of tipsy citizens who mount my rails settle
into my many creases where suns too
numerous to count have risen & set &
flash like my hazard orange nails which
seem to suggest there is only the present
danger of a life swallowing a life, a face
capsized caught between the bottle-
cap teeth of a giant squid, marked
like the sperm whale's face
is marked with overlapping rings
tattooed by the squid's suckers
scarred signature of prey
thwarting predator like
the signature of
the midge
in my throat.
My face knows
it's no different from
the midge. Knows not
to scrutinize the mirror if
it doesn't want to see its own
reflection if it doesn't want to see
a face steered into its own wake. If
it doesn't want to know the appetite
of rebel water, mercenary sunlight.

Executive Agenda

Each sentence, a mass-produced necklace clasped
at my throat like an heirloom

or a lasso—one of the cattle whose brain is also lateral.
Herded from pen to pasture to—

VP's!
The bottom
line's
shrinking
Who can
unpack from its
silo
an epic pep talk?

        I'm damp & twitchy, shy of fluorescence.
Who can zigzag me out of these corralled clauses?

I thought I was the handler.

tee up the synergy
vertically then
pluck the low-
hanging fruit accordingly
ripe
in your hands

I answer every red-exclamation-point question
with stock lexicon, strung, soldered.

Wake-up, not
a drill, an
Emergency! Our
playing field's 24/7
you must skate
to where the
puck's going to be

Easy to panic:

By day's end I'm a city sunset in a swivet
seen through a C-suite's tall windows.

Merely a mimic. What of my own notes?

They're as remote as a bird's nest made of spit strands,
glued to the cleft of a cave abutting the world's

most inaccessible beaches. They're a lucrative quarry:
Theft's epidemic. Despite the cave's reek

& high-risk limestone cliff, the black
market's remarkably bullish. Even if

I switch places with the swiftlet, gain
flight capability, I'd be no less endangered—

—even at night when I roost I'm on
board with moving the dial, the needle, please piggyback at your—

I flit my dream's hallways & elevators in stockings & suit.
Even in flight I'm perpetually meeting.

The Color Designer's Assignment to Herself

Name the color: reed
           grass in day-
                     break light, day
                               that means

to rain. Past
           flowering, flowers
                     intact: Pantone's
                               Smoke White. Grass past

human height. Cinched
           at the waist, so
                     the postman
                               doesn't have

to bushwhack.
           Sky contused
                     confused she
                               procrastinates.

No code
           matches it.
                     Is it love or the wish
                               for love that tints the grass?

My Father's Paycheck

In bird currency, one worm split among
        three children, a wife. Down in the bargain

basement of the bargain store, the bird nearly
        suicides in florescent light. Down here,

the sky's oneiric, the bird—panicked—swats
        through the clowder, claws a brunette—

a discontinued Barbie, skin incandescent—
        and drops her down my throat.

That Kind of Mouse

Chronic exposure to microwave radiation increases the rate of tumor growth in mice. The same increase occurs in chronically stressed mice that have never been exposed to radiation.

1.

Yes, I'm that kind of mouse.

I wash my tail with my teeth.
Saw it like a knife through tough meat.

It's bred into me
and my offspring. They barber their bodies too.

You don't need lab glasses to spot the bald patches.

I spit my paws & wash my face with spit, excessively.
It's worse in solitary,

a Plexiglas cube no bigger than me.
Released I attempt to outrun it—myself?—on a wire wheel

and for a few seconds, back flat, free—
I feel what they feel—the other mice

happily sniffing each other, yawning with equanimity.

2.

Hey you, with the lab coat—I'm more

than a control variable:
What about me?

I could be statistical
improbability.

I could be the milk of the null hypothesis.
I'm albino: I could be

the stillness of snow, milk pierced from a tree.
Don't underestimate me.

3.

I turn from the wheel to the window.
Snow pours, milk from a cloud.

Don't underestimate me.

I could be snow eloped with a river.
Or the river's reflection, walking on trees.

I could be the willow it walks on.
I have to start somewhere.

Burrowed under wood shavings, fur
infused with the fragrance of trees:

I could be a mouse with a deciduous happiness.

Run-Over Squirrel

We stop not because he's dead, but because he's dead on
        Vernon Street, where so little happens outside houses.
            Because he's broken open—

scarlet, vermillion? Here we stand at the edge
        of the visible spectrum, a man and a woman
            out for a walk in the black pastures

of the murderous suburbs. The squirrel, an old-world
        sacrifice, draws us out of our bodies, out
            of our separate minds. It must

have just happened, given the chromatic
        collision of beauty and violence. Arsenic,
            the covert ingredient in fifteenth century

Venetian red. By the sixteenth the Aztecs'
        cochineal, parasitic insect, crushed
            the European dye market. Cabbalistic,

cryptic red, reserved for cardinals, princes, bankers,
        courtesans. Translated through a Vernon Street
            window: sun-shot shoulder, flash

of a satin strap. The squirrel's blood now a hit-
        and-run red. I finger my
            dangling ruby earring like a rosary.

My Vestigial Shell

I was a small baby with a fat mother. Fat father too.
  Late in life I imitate them:
    A thin woman, stick arms, stick

legs with a doughy belly to remind me where
  I come from, how I mound & rise
    like yeast, mouthing

the damp heat, teething the gummy darkness.
  When I can't sleep, the fat woman wakes.
    She adores insomniacs, their amnesic

night eating. Lit by the fridge, the hundred
  blue eyes of a left-over scallop feast
    on my naked body. And look who's

here: my mother, pining as usual, among the caked
  gravy & gray marbled steak. Even
    in death, a wistful woman gristled

with need. She peers over a rubber-banded
  bunch of spinach, her plump
    tongue starved for company:

I'm a plate she wants to lick clean.
  I'm sympathetic but unwilling.
    Where is my father? Why

doesn't he put on his one good suit
  and fill up her dance card?
    Splayed like a side of meat over

a lawn chair, blue eyecups
      propped on his eyeballs, he turns on
            the spit of his basted belly, roasting.

Beside him, a towering Dagwood sandwich composed
      from every luncheon meat known to man,
            sour pickles & sweet gherkins,

horseradish, mayo, mustard. I'm lucky
      my father's no polar bear, or he'd eat me too:
            He wouldn't know any better.

When I was an infant, I was bathed
      in a colander. I've retained a remnant like
            the slug's vestigial shell, I drag it

wherever I go. No matter what
      I eat or drink, I'm never satisfied:
            Everything pours right through me.

Accounting: Monday Morning

Hard to yank from sleep to swallow
Monday's meager spoonful, dress

in requisite polish, instead of what's
tossed on the floor night before—
who we are shed of uniform.
                              Crammed in
the subway, I make
myself tiny as
possible.
Close my eyes,

daydream Nebraska's grasslands, twenty thousand square miles, where cattle
    run free.

Free?
That's daydream accounting.

In the actual grassland, each animal branded.
Like that bull I'm not capital, I'm labor.

Warm-blooded, bred for a higher rung, what
a fall by the time I
catch on I'm
equal

to the weight of my biweekly paycheck.
Assets insufficient, I'm a rough
estimate, not a certainty,
                              confetti
at the feet of the One-Percenters.

I'm a human bristling the skin I'm
enclosed in—what's my place

in the operation? I fill
with milk.

Side View of the Creative Director

Like a long-legged spoonbill, she slips
into the office thicket. Behind

paper-clipped leaves, she recedes.
Fit models wander, limbs loose

as sunlight. Perfectly apportioned,
Susie & Wendy, Chantelle, lovely

animals. Side to side her bill sweeps,
cheeks pink as the creatures she eats.

The Human Resources Director Muses on Ants

Ants are eusocial. They don't mind
following a leader's scent, single-file, down

a narrow corridor in pursuit of an objective.
Nor do they have to deal with everyone's

need to be special. Collectively intelligent,
ants don't project old hurts onto fellow ants.

Farmers, herders, slavers, they're more
like Homer's Greeks: all about action.

Ants belong to the order of wasps and bees,
though most no longer have wings.

Far older than our two hundred thousand years,
they arrived with the Giganotosaurus,

Iguanodon. They milk aphids like cows
for their honeydew, the caterpillars

of the blue butterfly for their nectar.
Creating their own paradox, ants traffic

in children, stealing young to care
for their young. They've colonized every

land mass except Antarctica (hah!
not eponymous)—and a few inhospitable

islands. Polynesia, Iceland, Hawaii.
No wonder scientists revere them—

each ant a flake falling in the form
of an Icelandic blizzard, a high-pitch

unity our office will never achieve.

That Kind of Human

1.

I'd cup her in a latex-free palm if I could,
stroke her bald patches.

I'd remove her from solitary.
From a Plexiglas tomb to a cage with a wheel,

but only temporarily. As if what
soothed her could soothe me.

I pick at my face. Like her, I pull
out my hair mercilessly.

The odds dead against her,
but what about me?

I'm not a control variable.
What about chance?

2.

What about water walking on trees?
Bird nests appearing like coins

from fistfuls of leaves?
By chance I'm garbed in a lab coat,

its canvas sleeves long enough
to knot my own crossed arms

behind my back. I test probability.
What's true for the mice

could be true for you and me.
After hours I study escapology.

Methodical as a mouse plotting
its moves behind a hedgerow—

Abracadabra! I'm gravity-free.

THE DROP RACK

Fashions of the Times

In August, we prep next Spring's collection.
Hundreds of garments shipped by air,

by ocean. From Shanghai, silk georgette,
from Mumbai, habutai. With only a week

to assemble Spring's stories, we're
immersed as forsythia branches, forced

to bloom early. Converged from multiple
floors onto one, we're an insect hum.

We hang, steam, mirror-preen this top,
that cardigan. One makes a flash-card face

that signifies displeasure; in the mirror
assenting flash-card faces rank, measure.

The garment found wanting, discarded.
Only those deemed most beautiful or

business-suitable avoid the drop rack.

✂

When I was a girl, when it counted (or
seemed to count) I was *out*. Friendless in frocks

that missed Glamour's mark, a weed
amongst fragrant hyacinth, waxy flowers

that colonize into cliques. Now, I'm
the one who decides what's In.

✂

Why mix confession with profession?
Fashion is shallow? Do you want me to argue

its function? (We have to wear clothes,
cajoled by weather or legal obligation).

Argue its intellectual vigor, design rigor?
Designers, merchandisers possessed,

obsessed, not with vanity (maybe
a little) but with recrudescent beauty.

The crocus, the daffodil, wake the sleeping
husk of a garment, wake its equivalent:

Spring opens its eyelid, detonates skin, kick-
starts the hum within—we're a song again.

✂

From the hum of land: flax, cotton.
From the sea: lustrous abalone buttons.

From sheep, featherweight merino. From oil,
thread. A designer draws a dress in her head.

The dress seeks a body to inhabit, make
itself complete, completes the body it sheathes.

✂

Here on Fifth Avenue as if biologically
driven, spring after spring we design

a collection. Start with fabric, color,
swatches pinned: double-weave, délavé

blue as a dragonfly's thorax. Cross-
dyed silk, even under fluorescence

a humming bird wing's iridescence.
A ropey tape yarn sheeny as milkweed

as creamy (pod cracked open, seeds
parachuting). Lest we get sidetracked

by the release our hearts mimic,
we layer on business analytics:

What sold last year, what didn't.

✄

I've clocked twenty Spring seasons. Can
I still claim the job accidental, counterfeit?

The out-girl's desire to be in appears
permanent. Each season, clothes I get for free

bagged, jump-shot in a Goodwill bin.
Nothing to do with will or goodness, just

making room for new stuff. To feed the lack
I clamp in my mouth like a lottery ticket.

✂

Out was what those three teen-girl
jihadists wanted, crossing Gatwick

security to meet kismet. Ditched
in the rest room, skinny pants, faux

leopard vest; consigned to their parents,
their alibis. In New York we adorn

perfectly proportioned, optic white
mannequins, rig next Spring's collection.

✂

Spring's first delivery, the end of February,
snow still fleet, our job to make spring

clothes irresistible long before its heat,
to conceal what makes her feel incomplete:

She thinks her breasts too round, too flat,
hips too large, butt too slack, calves too skinny,

too fat. Each with the parts she'd disinherit:
Better if we were uniformed, if our eyes,

lids lined with kohl, lashes, only sought
through the slot of black, crocheted mesh?

✂

Last year we borrowed the harem pant,
though not the harem. This year, those

most trendy wrap variations-on-a-turban.
First worn by Sultans, Wazirs, made its way

to the Continent to Vermeer. To whatever
it is we seek when we fall into the Girl

with a Pearl Earring. When we wrap
our heads like her, we're merely on trend,

magazine tear, pin-up. Drawn like butterflies
to a red wavelength's nectar, we flit culture

✂

to culture. Like the tulip from the wild
to the Ottoman Empire elite: palace

garden centerpiece, sketched in ink
engraved in pottery. In silk, poetry, its

motif brocaded. Height of court fashion,
a cut tulip tucked in the fold of a turban.

Thanks to diplomatic etiquette, seeds
flit west to Rome's royal botanist.

Two hundred years after, the populace
deemed the hyacinth Europe's most popular.

I fly on the fast track, crazed as
a tulipomaniac. In Turkey the tulip still

revered, perseveres, spray painted jet-side
on its eponymous airline. Seen through

silver petals, three faces: the Bethnal
Green, girl teens land in Istanbul.

✄

Live from the mood board, the double
late-flowering Angelique: Float over

a white slip dress in linen its mirror
dress in blush organza. Pair with a pale

pink cardigan, wafer-thin that collapses
against her skin—she the tulip we merchandise.

Like this spring, next spring we'll each
think we're unique, yet we'll look like

each other, petal pink planted in suites
of threes and fives to naturalize, repeat.

✄

As a house finch in August flies
to a sunflower hedge, furiously feasting

from oversized heads. After hours
caught, like a seed's black oil in my beak,

in the dimly-lit dark, in the quiet
I confess: I shop the drop rack.

In parallel someone snaps a shot
on a cell in a local park: From the back

like starlings flocked, three girls side-
by-side garbed in head-to-toe black.

THE SAME HARMONIC

Would a Fifth Century Greek Stop

in his sandaled tracks, gawk
like me, at the morning's discourse—

six a.m., each-and-every white hull
in the harbor, sun-swacked?

Citizen of a gift economy, would
he think it a gift as I do, though

I'm subject to the laws of currency?
White's degree of brightness

nearly violent & though absolutely
silent—magnified, mallet-stung,

the day's gong. Chalk white,
writes on me, declining my wound

up anonymity, declining my
mind spun at high speed like

a souvenir sweatshirt zipper
coiled in a coin dryer. The Greek

wouldn't seek equanimity in
the harbor's blinding (would he?).

Wouldn't hear the halyards
as tempo—just banging.

In the fleet, he wouldn't see
a grove of coruscating trees, but

symmetry shining. And me?
Waves break & enter my mind's

periphery, its foamy debris, till
my self's audible as the view

I purchased, till I'm convinced
the bay's salty lick signifies.

Like Capital

I circulate. By express train, by taxi,
      by town car, I become the millennial

night in the same hotel, a Mylar bouquet,
      1-0-0-0, with its silver vine staked

from headboard to ceiling: strobe lights, spider
      mums, cheese & fruit plate, an excess

of optimistic objects. I become a plug number,
      residing in a cell in the hotel's P&L.

Monday through Thursday, foiled chocolate,
      my highlighted hair rests in down pillows

that point west to the Hudson. My child,
      my husband a dream asleep in a valley

with a high pollen count, my self a credit
      to the universe, cashless. Early mornings,

no one at the office, I stare out from my
      singular body at a wooden water tower.

A village feeling atop a stone & steel building.
      Roused as if from another life, one

I would have lived more elementally. Below, evenly
      spaced, specimen trees measure the streets.

Apocalypse in Two Parts

I watch a pair of Asiatic beetles
with their orange-enameled wings, gnaw
a swath of white lilies—every petal, leaf,
till the swath—the world?—is skeletal.
They're mating. Two-for-one
I cage them between palms, relish
their oversize shrieks.

When you come, the wind blows your
words of instruction down a passing beach, out
to sea. The word *strap* never
reaches my ears, the word *winch.*
I'm no boat—you can't pull me out.
Instead I release the swarm of words that
fill my head, till I'm bees by the thousands
feeding off every flower head.

I Was the 60s Becoming the 70s

Selectrically typing for Mr. Whosit & Whatsit,
calculators of the worst-case scenario—
I was a Temporary Girl. A by-the-hour,

by-the-week girl. An eighty-five-words-
per-minute girl. College girl fated to type
the summer by form, by rote, by deadline

in the carpeted forests of hushed receptions,
while palm trees lined the boulevards
of Hollywood & other hopefuls wandered

its promising, fraudulent light. I earned
my keep under fluorescence. Kali
under wraps, with my blue cheeks & eight

arms to answer phone lines, I practiced
a pleasant demeanor—already
past *1-2-3-4 we don't want your*

fucking war. Past the beach bonfire—
kids lost in each other's tongues,
I alone witnessed man's moon step.

My best friend came home Born
Again, but I was already taken
by Meher Baba, his business card

sleek in my T-Girl pocket, with
its dorm room instruction:
Don't worry, be happy.

My friend's hair poured across the pier
like La Niña. Each of us
entering different kingdoms.

La Florida Paradise

Nocked, strung, I'm the arrow shot
into a crimson pool flowering
in the pine flats, bull's-eye

that erupted after hard rain. Rain that we—
spontaneous, strangers, soaked, nearly
naked—boogied into. As always,

before & since, an attempt to shake self-
consciousness out through
hips and shoulders, a violent twist-

ing like the heads of wet dogs.
At eighteen who wouldn't be wet
with the wish to fake-out

the pack around you?
On that bright day, my free,
my floating anxiety flaunted

its counterfeit buoyancy, an arrow
fletched, drawn from a distance
in that land foreign with sand spurs.

At eighteen a swimmer who couldn't
resist a new pool. Too late, *cher bébé*,
to realize its jeweled surface wasn't

water, wasn't *La Florida* yet to
discover, but a raft made by fire
ants, latched to each other, latching

onto me. And here they still are,
in memory: their carnelian crust, their
venom about to seep into my skin.

And here I still am, the gullible,
the hopeful arrow that
flies toward them.

Evolution

Descendant of the theoretically
        questionable aquatic gorilla, I jump

into a flotilla of eel grass awash
        with amphibious happiness, my

bipedal heart clamoring to converge
        with the origin of its own question.

In the International Dark Zone

"Okay Ranger," says the silk voice in my skull: "Do your stuff.
　　　　Do your awe & wonder."
　　　　　　　　　　We lie like patients in snowy gowns

beneath the smeared stars of the Milky Way, as it scans
　　　　the soft tissues of our bodies, our downy hunks & drifts lying

side by side spanning the tarmacked view overlooking Zabriskie Point.
　　　　We've come to decipher the sky guaranteed starry

by the Dark Sky Association. Out here there are no city towers
　　　　for bird flocks to strike.
　　　　　　　　　　"Paladins of the Night,"

the Ranger commands, *"Switch off your flashlights."*
　　　　A million oxygen masks release from the star-punctured sky.

Radio waves pass through me, as if tuned to read & reveal my most
　　　　arrestable self. I'm far west of my day job

where it's back-to-back meetings,
　　　　perpetually florescent. Restless, electric,
　　　　　　　　　　I crackle, static on satin.

The Big Dipper scrubs me like tinfoil in a washing machine.
　　　　With her laser, the Ranger tracks Orion's conspicuous belt,

the dissolute W of Cassiopeia, but when she moves on to more
　　　　erudite citings:
　　　　　　　　　　"Plot a line between Taurus & Leo,

due north of the intersect, Castor & Pollux..."
  she's lost the near-sighted among us. My naked eyes shut.

I lie & listen as her voice detaches & falls like a star. Still,
  peace eludes me. "Ranger," says the electromagnetically weary

voice in my skull, "Too bright to see what I'm thinking or feeling.
  What I've forfeited. I'm
              shorting: like a bird

      trying to fly through a window.
          Where's the socket, the fuse box, the breaker?"

Fear Refuses My Brisket & Hanukah Lights

With antipathy to miracles, its
serrated dog-lips want only
the raw, the wind-chapped me,

when the director talks
fast in my face, my
slender neck exposed

to her teeth. When my working
soul whirls like an anti-dervish
entranced with self-pity & its

cunning white caps
whipped to remind me
I'm the frenzied

nothing stamped under feet.
Until the nothing becomes
the bristle & bone of my grown

child's jaw in a waking yawn,
when he tugs my cheek
to his cheek—the wild

dogs deposed, can't
compete.

Thin Lips

I'm not attracted to men with thin lips, yet now
my husband, you have them. Pharmaceutically
fueled you sit on a sofa, stymied by a spreadsheet

as if it's an airlock to an alternate universe,
alternate Ed. The past never adds up. The present
intersects a future only as far as cash flows:

After that, life's a forfeit. With each tallied
failure your plush lips subtract themselves,
briny with the taste of a digital deficit.

You insist you're the failure: It's your coinage.
If it weren't for me we'd live in a lean-to.
Stalled by your neurological deficit, displaced

in your crust, you tap from a silver
vial your kiddie-coke cure for inertia. Your
vanishing lips merely one of its irreversible tricks.

No wonder you're dreaming your Florida boyhood,
the low-flying plane spraying strata of DEET
creamy as sleepwalking sheep—a cumulus cloud

you bike into following it like the future. Ever since
your life coming, then going. Nothing adds up.
Your toes want out of their toe box, they're

snapping, they're bunching & bucking. Even
at night they persist, a Morse SOS, nonrefundable
wish. Asleep, your lips lush. I kiss them awake.

My lips are tender as money: Between us, no deficit.

Gassed Up

At the Mobile station on Route 95, above
hidden lawns & property lines, the descending
sun democratized. An unpremeditated state

on the rise. Numb after the workweek,
lost in my head, body a stump—stinging
its edges a peculiar sensation—

                              gratitude

cut on the horizon line, cheap
& abundant as boxed wine. Its drunken
practice advertised by church, by state,

poseurs of the wise. The sun's notes
score the sky, the frequency shifts.
Merely weeks till the indiscernible peepers

chime in. At the gas pump, my throat
inflates, my arms unaccountably rise—
crowned chartreuse, devoured by light.

My legs take their time from the car
down the mini-mart's snack aisle, brushing
humanity's thighs. End of the workweek,

empty-headed, leafy, loosely pinned to the sky.

Beach Debris

That I could prove as Galileo did:
my self, like the Earth
is not the fixed center of
the universe
but one revolving bit
seen through
this tiny toy telescope today's
low tide tenders.
I long for a telescopically
neutral view of my own
tiny galaxy—
my own life, I mean.
Younger, hungry
for ideas, I admired Kepler's
music of the spheres, planets
humming, us tuned
to the same harmonic.
Now this self-
preoccupation. No break
from the fricative fire
my own mind makes.
A league of salt
& seven heavenly
realms to penetrate
before the fire's satisfied.

New Year's Ledger 2014

This year's celeb dead tallied, catalogued, glossy
as we near the finish line. Never mind

the ongoing wars (nom du jour conflicts)
the confusing acrostic of factions, fractions,

acronyms, each with its signature violence.
This week, an auld lang syne to the top

twenty most popular bygone, vanished
from the cul-de-sac of an era. This year's

exception to type, war reporter James Foley:
beheaded celebrity.
                        No matter how famous,

you have to drop dead by the deadline.
If you sip your last breath between Christmas

and New Year's, you slide like a coin
into a meter that eats what it's fed between

this year and next. If you're still on the grid
of the living, the list's unavoidable, sung from

each hillside, poured through ear buds or
cued up on coffee tables. Gone Ms. Becall's

Belarus glamour my mother copied.
Gone Shirley Temple (FDR's little darling)—

orphaned rain who soaked the Reffe's
with the belief we too could tap dance into

love and money. Reading entry after entry,
impossible not to concede the inky

accounting. I've lived long enough to know
my life as the treasure the tiniest hand

once retrieved from a cereal box, tracked
in a ledger shopkeepers use, textured

to imitate leather. Engraved on its
cover: "Beat Yesterday" in gold letters.

March Wednesday

           I'm obsessed with the future, the one
      with dandelions that metastasize like

multiple-choice bad endings:
        My heart a fisted hyacinth
           refusing to open one morning,

or, *ha, ha,* tumorous bulbs detonating in my breasts,
        or, like the lily feasting red beetles,
            my bones turn to lace.

                Can anyone save me?

This week, the resurrection advertised, the future
        wrapped in a foiled chocolate egg
           I'd like to unpeel.

I don't know Jesus, though I've been told
        I'm one of his people. Once
           in a Florida church I even sang

in a white robe with gold embossed cross
        sheening from my breastbone
           to my belly, my mouth

        opened to receive the host
to see what He was like.

All my life I've been trying to resurrect.
        Little thrill of Jewish guilt.
           Apart from that, he tasted like saw dust.

Apart from that life went on, the future arriving, then passing.

What if I were one of the faithful? Today I'd
      line up for the sanctified thumb to cross
           my forehead with the ash of burnt palm leaves.

For forty days, cease & desist lamenting the henceforth
      and hereafter, the terminally-recurring tomorrow.

Wouldn't I take as a sign the end of last night's party,
      my body turned on its axis
           from latched door to dirt road,

           my parked car where I left it, altered
      as the road, transubstantiated
by snow falling in moonlight, my neck

tilted to receive each arrowed flake on my infidel tongue?

Acknowledgements

Katie Peterson and David Rivard: You are illuminators and true friends. For pushing and pushing some more—Sharon Dolin. To Erika Wright, poetry dowser, who helped divine the final order of this book. To Michaela Sullivan, for your spirit, for your bees. To Kathleen Winter, for selecting this manuscript, *seeing* it—and to Dana Curtis for seeing it first and for getting it into the light of day.

To the Fine Arts Work Center and Mass Cultural Council for early faith and support.

To Ed, Zeke and Claire—family.

Thank you to these magazines in which versions of these poems first appeared:

Witness and Poetry Daily	"My Life Shrinks to the Size of a Midge"
Riddle Fence	"New Year's Ledger 2014" and "Run-Over Squirrel"
Denver Quarterly	"Self Portrait in a Rental Kitchen" and "That Kind of Mouse."
Hotel Amerika	"Kink in the Polar Vortex," "The Zoanthropist," and "March Wednesday."
Public Poetry Anthology on Power	"The Executive Assistant's Astral Existence."

Photo by Robin Barber

CANDICE REFFE is a poet who worked in fashion in New York City for over twenty years. In 2012 she won the Launch Innovator award. As part of a collective CEO, she led impact and innovation strategies. She has twice been a fellow at the Fine Arts Work Center in Provincetown and was awarded a Mass Cultural Council Artist Fellowship. Her poems have appeared in *Ploughshares, Threepenny Review, Hotel Amerika, Poetry Daily, Witness,* and elsewhere. She lives in Northampton, MA.

ELIXIR PRESS TITLES

POETRY

Circassian Girl by Michelle Mitchell-Foust
Imago Mundi by Michelle Mitchell-Foust
Distance From Birth by Tracy Philpot
Original White Animals by Tracy Philpot
Flow Blue by Sarah Kennedy
A Witch's Dictionary by Sarah Kennedy
The Gold Thread by Sarah Kennedy
Rapture by Sarah Kennedy
Monster Zero by Jay Snodgrass
Drag by Duriel E. Harris
Running the Voodoo Down by Jim McGarrah
Assignation at Vanishing Point by Jane Satterfield
Her Familiars by Jane Satterfield
The Jewish Fake Book by Sima Rabinowitz
Recital by Samn Stockwell
Murder Ballads by Jake Adam York
Floating Girl (Angel of War) by Robert Randolph
Puritan Spectacle by Robert Strong
X-testaments by Karen Zealand
Keeping the Tigers Behind Us by Glenn J. Freeman
Bonneville by Jenny Mueller
State Park by Jenny Mueller
Cities of Flesh and the Dead by Diann Blakely
Green Ink Wings by Sherre Myers
Orange Reminds You Of Listening by Kristin Abraham
In What I Have Done & What I Have Failed To Do by Joseph P. Wood
Bray by Paul Gibbons
The Halo Rule by Teresa Leo
Perpetual Care by Katie Cappello
The Raindrop's Gospel: The Trials of St. Jerome and St. Paula by Maurya Simon
Prelude to Air from Water by Sandy Florian
Let Me Open You A Swan by Deborah Bogen
Cargo by Kristin Kelly
Spit by Esther Lee

Rag & Bone by Kathryn Nuerenberger
Kingdom of Throat-stuck Luck by George Kalamaras
Mormon Boy by Seth Brady Tucker
Nostalgia for the Criminal Past by Kathleen Winter
Little Oblivion by Susan Allspaw
Quelled Communiqués by Chloe Joan Lopez
Stupor by David Ray Vance
Curio by John A. Nieves
The Rub by Ariana-Sophia Kartsonis
Visiting Indira Gandhi's Palmist by Kirun Kapur
Freaked by Liz Robbins
Looming by Jennifer Franklin
Flammable Matter by Jacob Victorine
Prayer Book of the Anxious by Josephine Yu
flicker by Lisa Bickmore
Sure Extinction by John Estes
State Park by Jenny Mueller
Selected Proverbs by Michael Cryer
Rise and Fall of the Lesser Sun Gods by Bruce Bond
I will not kick my friends by Kathleen Winter
Barnburner by Erin Hoover
Live from the Mood Board by Candice Reffe

FICTION

How Things Break by Kerala Goodkin
Juju by Judy Moffat
Grass by Sean Aden Lovelace
Hymn of Ash by George Looney
Nine Ten Again by Phil Condon
Memory Sickness by Phong Nguyen
Troglodyte by Tracy DeBrincat
The Loss of All Lost Things by Amina Gautier
The Killer's Dog by Gary Fincke
Everyone Was There by Anthony Varallo
The Wolf Tone by Christy Stillwell